Edited by: Takara M. Carter
Illustrated by: Writluxe Writing Firm

Publisher
Writluxe Writing Firm
Murfreesboro, Tennessee 37130
www.writluxe.org
1-866-498-2101

The things
I wish to be...

My name is Laila and this story is about me.

My teacher taught me how to read and write, so an author is what I wish to be.

I want to write books for kids like you and me, and tell stories full of excitement and creativity.

Maybe I can be a nurse and help people who are sick.

I can use my writing skills to take notes.

I can help doctors with little kids who need help feeling better too.

If I work in the hospital, there is so much I can do.

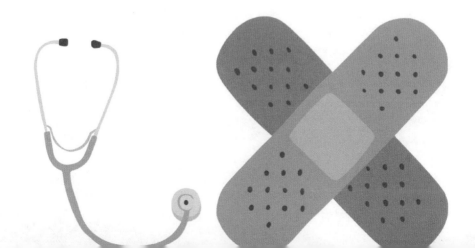

Or, I can create video games and be a professional player.

Kids can buy the games and play all day.

I can create games that help kids learn and play.

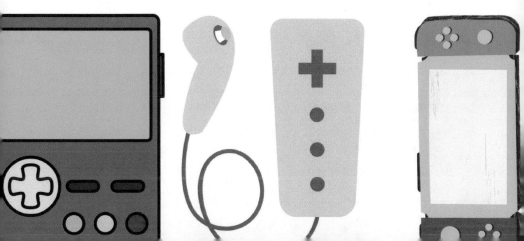

I also love music and want to play in the band.

I want to learn to play the Violin and piano with my friends.

I want to do a solo on stage for my family.

To show them how good music can be.

Maybe I can be a scientist. I can use beakers to mix things up and see the reaction.

I can read my books and learn about the planet. I want to learn how things work.

I can look at cells, molecules, and mix ingredients to even make slime.

I want to work on a farm and feed the animals. I can help them grow day by day.

I can feed them and give them baths. I can be outside with them and let them play in the grass.

My farm will have cows, sheep, ducks, and pigs.

I'll have squirrels, dogs, roosters and chickens.

I can become a teacher and help kids learn math. I can teach them their ABC's and how to read.

I can teach them how to study and do good in school.

I want to be a teacher and someday change the world too.

I can fight fires and save the city. I can even rescue my best friends kitten.

I can learn to climb trees and use the big water hose. I can teach people how to be safe, even at home.

I want to play sports too. I can be the next best baseball player.

I can work on my pitch and learn how to use my bat.

I have to also wear my uniform and my baseball hat. Maybe I can be famous doing that.

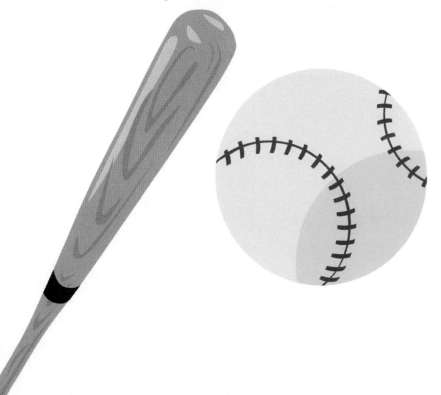

Most of all, I want to become a judge and help people like you and me. I want to fight for our equal rights.

I want to spread love and be fair to everyone, but I also want to protect people and show the the importance of doing good.

But first, I have to finish school and get a college degree. And hopefully someday, you and I will become all the things we wish to be.

I can do this

I believe in me

Made in the USA
Middletown, DE
20 December 2021

56691066R00015